WOBURN & ASPLEY GUISE
VINTAGE POSTCARDS

COMPILED AND EDITED

BY

PAUL COX

WOBURN AND ASPLEY GUISE VINTAGE POSTCARDS

Published by Paul Cox, 2021

ISBN 978-1-3999-0443-8

Copyright © Paul Cox

hogstyend@btinternet.com

Front cover: Top, a hand-tinted view across the Woburn rooftops to the new Church from the tower of the original Church, later used as a Mortuary Chapel and now Woburn Heritage Centre. Bottom, Tinted view of "The Steamer" beerhouse on West Hill, Aspley Guise. Opened by 1851, it was closed in 1927 after 33 years in the hands of licensees William and Johanna Lane.
Rear cover: A hand-tinted view into Aspley Guise Square from Chain House in Church Street by Herbert Gregory's Sandpine Press, c.1906.

CONTENTS

FOREWORD

Out on the western edge of the county of Bedfordshire, near the border with Buckinghamshire, lies the town of Woburn and the village of Aspley Guise.

Woburn is known internationally as the home of the Duke of Bedford and Russell family. Having been taken from the Cistercian monastic residents by Henry VIII and given to John Russell, 1st Earl of Bedford in 1547, it only became the Ducal home later, some say after his family moved out of London to avoid the deadly plagues of the 17th century. The original building was demolished and a new one erected on the same site, but the name 'Abbey' was retained. There are many books on the history of the Dukedom and Woburn Abbey; in this one, I shall be concentrating on the town itself.

Once a thriving market town, Woburn was an important trading and commercial centre for this area of Bedfordshire. It also stood on one of the principal coach routes to the Midlands. The main road through, from Watling Street at Hockliffe, was turnpiked in 1706 and used to reach the important shoe and leatherwork town of Northampton and beyond. These coaches brought visitors to Woburn who wanted services and refreshments during their stopover. Today, the main trade of Woburn is still traveller-based; tourists for the Abbey, the Safari Park and the world-renowned Woburn Golf Courses.

Access to the Abbey gardens and grounds was controlled by the various gatehouses and lodges, but limited tickets could be bought to enter from quite an early time. The fashionable Victorians and then Edwardians would come to spend the day wandering the locale and no doubt jotting off a quick postcard to let their friends know what a delightful time they were having.

In contrast to the fine Georgian buildings of Woburn, Aspley Guise is a far smaller and quieter place to the north, still on the periphery of Bedford Estate. The original name *Aspeleia* (in the Domesday book of 1086) derives from "Aspen lea" meaning "a clearing in the aspen" and was then extended in the late medieval period when Anselm de Gyse became Lord of the Manor in 1375. It owes its wealth and respectable reputation to several factors: the siting of a successful private Classical Academy from at least 1723; being on the road westwards from Bedford; having a halt on the Oxford to Cambridge line and because Dr James Williams recommended the village as a health resort for recovering T.B. patients in the 1850s. It was a much cheaper alternative to sending sufferers abroad to warmer and drier climes.

Although quite different in their demographic, both places had visitors wanting to send messages home. Postcards were also used by locals wanting to send a quick message to family, friends or businesses. With several collections from post boxes daily, a local card could reach its destination the same day. The picture postcard craze really took off after 1902, when Post Office regulations first allowed a message and address to share one side of the card, meaning a large picture could occupy the other. They became a cheap attractive collectable that could be displayed in decorative albums to show others where you had been and what you had done; the Edwardian version of a social media feed!

Coinciding with the eras of cheaper travel and more free time, postcards allowed people to see the far-off places that they may never have been able to visualise. Illustrations in books and newspapers were still mainly sketches. As photographic equipment became more readily available, everywhere had a budding photographer producing studio portraits. Sitters still had to remain quite still for a length of time so as not to blur the image. This is why most early postcard views do not include passers-by.

Postcards remained popular until after the First World War and the advent of instantaneous communication via the telephone. They have survived at the seaside as an enduring part of the British psyche connected to visiting new places and wanting to tell friends and family what a nice time you are having.

Woburn's postcards tend to centre of the crossroads and the two main roads through the town. Aspley Guise has many more lanes and views spread over a greater area, meaning there are actually more postcards of it than Woburn. I have been collecting local cards for 30 years and I am indebted to the other local collectors and residents who have shared what they have. Following the success of my book *Woburn Sands, Aspley Heath and Wavendon Vintage Postcards* last year, these are some of the cards published of Woburn and Aspley Guise. I hope you enjoy looking at the scenes of life from 100 years ago.

As I said before, *"Wish you were here!"*

Paul Cox, 2021.

WOBURN - SOUTH TO NORTH

The Grand Entrance, Woburn Abbey

GRAND ENTRANCE WOBURN PARK

When coming along London Road from Hockliffe, the first indication that you are about to enter a place of substance is this imposing gateway. The Grand Entrance to Woburn Park is a statement of wealth and importance. The 100-metre-long concave entrance to Woburn Park for official visitors was completed in 1810 for John, 6th Duke of Bedford, with Henry Holland and Humphry Repton having a hand in it.

It meant visitors to the Duke did not have to pass the town. The top card, published by Pikesley's Post Office at Woburn Sands, was sent locally to Mr. Jones at New Cottage, Woburn in 1909. The one left is unsent, but sold by Fisher & Sons, the Woburn printer and stationers.

Paris House stands inside the London Gate. This description is provided by the restaurant now based there: *"...originally built in 1878 as part of the Paris International Exhibition on the Rue des Nations in Paris. The 9th Duke of Bedford fell in love with it, had it dismantled, shipped piece by piece and rebuilt in the stunning grounds of Woburn Abbey".* It has been a tonsil hospital and safehouse for Winston Churchill when he visited Bletchley and then a restaurant since 1983.

A clear view, by photographer Robert Cheetham of Woburn Sands, showing Ivy Lodge, a more 'ordinary' way into Woburn Park for visitors on foot, but still one thought to have been designed by Humphry Repton in the early 19th century. I wonder what they called it before the ivy grew up? Unsent, but c.1905-10.

A view further along London Road towards Woburn, postally used in 1913. The nine miles of redbrick wall surrounding this part of Woburn Park, right, was started in 1792.

A young girl has seen the photographer, Cheetham again, so being captured for eternity. In the background, the signboard for the Royal Oak is hanging on the wall of the white-ended building, centre-left of the view, with that for the White Hart beerhouse on a post almost dead centre. Unsent.

This nicely embossed card has the unusual address of "Woburn, Bletchley". That was the nearest main Post Office at one time and letters so directed would arrive earlier than ones through Bedford. The Royal Oak has suffered several fires in the thatch over the years. It is now an Italian restaurant. An unused card, the signboard is a classic Wells & Winch Brewery of Biggleswade c.1950s-60s design.

A modern-ish view of George Street, c.1977, by Duck Lane. The house on the right is Bedford House (once Crowholt) and the gable-end now features a golden Russell family crest, with their motto *"Che Sera Sera"* - "Whatever will be, will be".

An unusual private-house card, probably made for the owner. This building is no.14 George Street, opposite "The Woburn" hotel. The sender asked S. Lewis of 5 Rutland Road, Bedford *Do you recognise this?"* on 11th May 1909.

The hotel has had several names. It was the George (hence George Street), the Bedford Arms and the Inn at Woburn. It was once a Trusthouse Forte hotel. The billhead below is from 1858.

BEDFORD ARMS HOTEL, WOBURN, BEDS.
Proprietor: Jas. G. Walker.

A card produced for James Walker, who was licensee here 1902-09, no doubt to sell to guests. A later landlord, Mr. F. Ward, (1911-13), obviously inherited the unsold stock and simply wrote his name over the top of his predecessor! Used in 1911.

This shot shows the building beside the hotel, left, once Wiffen's ironmongery and later under Gibson Andrew. It was demolished in 1919 and used for the Woburn War Memorial site. This card was sent in 1906 to Fenny Stratford.

A good view of the demolished building that once stood opposite. Unsent, (but post-First World War as the Memorial is erected) Hulatt's tailor & livery maker's shop, centre-right, stands on an area which is grass now. It was demolished in the 1930s.

We come to the main crossroads, a favourite stop for all postcard photographers. To the right of the Town Hall stands a captured German artillery gun, given to the Duke after the First World War by the Bedfordshire Regt. It was taken for scrap during the Second, so this postcard, used in 1947, was already out of date.

The edge of Andrew's ironmongers, with his display of spades and tinware, is just caught on this card by Herbert Gregory of Woburn Sands. The neatly bollard-ed Pitchings are still there. Plenty of room to leave your cart whilst shopping!

I am not sure one lady on a bicycle warranted two policemen to direct traffic! Many windows in Woburn are only painted onto buildings, including the first floor of the building on the right. This lessened the payments of Window Tax, imposed on houses with more than 10, in the 1700s.

The top middle window of Gilby's general drapey is also painted on. This card by Gregory of Woburn Sands was posted, but sadly a stamp collector has removed the evidence of the postmark and date. It was sent to "The Misses Litchfield, Aspley Guise, Local" to show them where the sender lived.

From the Bedford & County Record, 12th January 1900:

"*Woburn - Where to shop. An enterprising firm of drapers and outfitters, Messrs McKay Bros. business in the Market Square is thoroughly up-to-date. Every department is distinguished by the keynote of efficiency and customers have always every reason to be satisfied alike with the moderate price and the high quality of Messrs. McKay's goods. In a district such as Woburn an ironmonger's stores manifestly meets a real want. Certainly Mr. J. Peelings are so admirably stocked that it would be difficult to mention something connected with an ironmonger's or allied trade which he does not supply. His multifarious goods comprise in addition to ironmongery proper, cutlery, jewellery, guns and pistols, china, glass and earthen-ware and the many requisites connected with cycling. Mr. W. Janes is a practical and competent watch and clock maker. His shop also contains many useful and fancy articles while his versatility is shown by the energy with which he is acting as agent for the famous Dunlop tyres and for all cycle accessories. Mr. Lilley is a leading confectioner who conducts his business on hygienic principles. Consequently the bread, pastry and other dainties procurable at his shop are the perfection of flavour and purity.*"

TOWN HALL AND MARKET SQUARE. WOBURN.

The Town Hall, built in 1830 for John, 6th Duke, was designed by Edward Blore and replaced an earlier version. The English Heritage Grade II listing notes that the structure is "*in a loosely Jacobethan style*". It had its own full-time keeper and the upstairs was once a large lofty hall available for parish events. Undated card by Fisher & Sons.

A very animated scene, sent in August 1917 to Leicester. After his shop next to the hotel was demolished, Gibson Andrew moved his business to nos. 8, 9 & 10 Market Place, now the China Shop.

A horse and cart waits patiently outside Andrew's ironmongers c.1906. Before his business there, it had been in the same trade under John and Elizabeth Wiffen, parents of the noted Society of Friends' poet Jeremiah and writer Benjamin.

The Town Hall, Woburn
Copyright Wbn. 3
Raphael Tuck & Sons Ltd London

Gilby's name is still over the door of 19 Market Place here, as it had been 50 years before this postcard was taken in the late 1950s. Closer to the camera is Florence Champkin's confectioners and Dudeney & Johnston grocer's, who also had stores in Woburn Sands and elsewhere in Bedfordshire.

Park Street & War Memorial, Woburn

Henry Fisher's printing works gets a number of mentions in this book. Here is an excellent view of his newsagent's shopfront on the corner of Park Street. Unused, but this must be after 1919, by which time his son had taken it over. If only the Police were there directing traffic now...

Left, the local section of the London to Northampton, Derby and Manchester coach route through Woburn, printed in 1785.

A trip could be booked on Messrs. E. Sharman & Co.'s coach, *"The Telegraph"* in 1836, departing from the "Bull & Mouth" in St Martins-le-Grand. The entire trip took 18½ hours, with four passengers inside in relative comfort and 11 clinging to the top! Another service by W. Chaplin & Co. left the "Swan with Two Necks" in Lad Lane and took 22½ hours. The breaks to change horses would have been a very welcome relief from the juddering coaches, badly sprung, on rough road surfaces. The Toll roads might be reasonable in some places, but much of it wasn't.

Lord Torrington stayed at the George Hotel (as was) in 1789. He wrote: *"We were well treated at the George, but were charged as we have been unaccustomed to, in the grand tavern style…"*

The George was the only 'proper' coaching inn in Woburn. Here the well-paying traveller could be put up and fed. Those of a lower class (or less funds) had a large variety of other inns and public houses to seek shelter at. There were 16 listed in 1823.

Right, the tariff for the Bedford Arms from 1937.

BEDFORD ARMS HOTEL, WOBURN.
Telephone 208.
(Hot and cold water in bedrooms)

TARIFF

		£	s.	d.
Single Bedroom and Breakfast, per night		0	8	6
Double Bedroom and Breakfast, per night		0	15	6
Twin-bedded Room and Breakfast, per night		0	17	0
Luncheon	2/6 and	0	3	6
Afternoon Tea		0	1	3
Dinner	3/6 and	0	4	6
En Pension Terms, per week (Available for a stay of five days or over)		4	4	0
Week-end Terms, not available Bank Holiday Week-ends (Including Dinner or Supper on Friday and Breakfast on Monday)		1	17	6
EXTRAS. Early Morning Tea		0	0	6
Service of Meal in Bedroom		0	0	6
Garage overnight		0	1	6

En Pension and Week-end Terms must be claimed when the room is booked.

PROPRIETORS - - TRUST HOUSES LTD.

12

From a time when there were no bollards around the Pitchings at all. Perhaps the caravaner is on the way to one of the many Caravanning Club events held in Woburn Park during the 1950-60s.

The Pitchings end just on the left. Another evocative shot of a shop's wares outside on the pavement. Three intrepid cyclists are just arriving, resplendent in their boaters. Perhaps they will call into the Black Horse for refreshment, right. The boys with the puppy are more interested in the camera. c.1910.

A selection of local billheads and advertisement cards. Turney's grocers was at 11 Market Place; Draper John Ibbott Slinn, also of the Market Place, died in 1872; Joseph Sergeant, stationer, sold out to Henry Fisher in 1897. Clarke's Wheat Protector was one of two such firms locally, along with Down's Farmer's Friend.

Woburn.

One last look back at the centre. A Beds Series card pre-1919. Bollards as big as the boys! There was once an open lane leading along the backs of the houses on Market Square which came out just to the right of this shot.

OLD GRAMMAR SCHOOL AND CHURCH. WOBURN.

The school on Bedford Street was founded by Francis, 2nd Earl of Bedford in July 1582. He conveyed to trustees a piece of land *"on which a house for a free school is erected"*.

In Woburn parish registers, under the heading *"Bury'd of the plague anno domini 1625"* is listed James Tong, master of the free school, with five of his children. It was listed in October 1952 as Grade II, of special interest. The listing notes that the original building was reworked around 1830 by Edward Blore. The large doors were the entrance for Woburn Fire Station from 1755-1947, when a purpose-built building in Leighton Street was erected.

Card unsent, part of the local Fisher & Sons series.

15

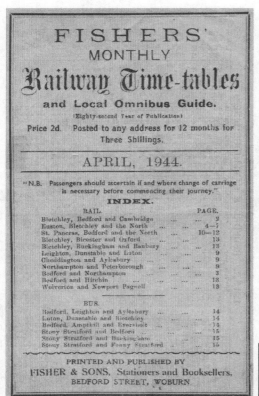

We can find out much about postcard publisher, printer and stationer Henry George Fisher from his 1909 obituary in the Beds. Times. He was apprenticed in 1857 to Dodd & Peeling, the Woburn printers. He then established a partnership with Henry Rush in Leighton Street. The business thrived and moved to Park Street. He then set up his own business in the High Street in 1868. He had eight children, including Henry John Fisher, who became the Postmaster of Woburn.

In public life, he was a member of the School Board and Parish Council; director of the Woburn Gas Company; trustee to the Woburn charities; deacon and secretary of the Congregational Church; and he took a prominent part in the temperance movement from its commencement.

He purchased the local printing and stationery business of Joseph Sergeant in 1897, afterwards taking his eldest son into partnership; and in 1907 acquired the printing business of Hulatt & Richardson in Bedford.

"In both business and private life he exhibited a marked degree of courtesy and consideration, and in his death the town loses yet another of its rapidly dwindling old-time tradesmen."

His son Henry John took over the business and kept the name 'Fisher & Sons' going.

Right, an advert from the 1944 timetable booklet above.

What is the meaning of the code on this card, when the visitor had been at Woburn possibly? I doubt they would have noticed much of a difference between 1883 and 1925! It is in unused condition, looking back along Bedford Street. In 1925, 14 Bedford Street, left, was the shop of butcher Francis J. Negus.

Another classical building on Bedford Street is the Old Parsonage, here seen on a card used in 1918. Sent to a Mrs. Stratford in Tring to say the sender had enjoyed their visit but left her gloves behind and perhaps they would stay longer next year. The Parsonage may have been built around an earlier building on the same site.

A very similar view to the last but in 1935. The Black Horse signboard is to the right. The first mention of this at Bedfordshire Archives is from 1743 when a Widow Clark of the Black Horse appears in a list of those owing dues to the Vicar. At this point, it was run by the brewery J. W. Green Ltd., of Luton.

Bedford Street, Woburn   KN 22258

The Sixties were as Swingin' in Woburn as elsewhere in Britain. There was a hippy *Festival of the Flower Children* at Woburn Park in August 1967 and Jimi Hendrix played there in July 1968, with Tyrannosaurus Rex and John Mayall's Bluesbreakers in support. I doubt Woburn had seen such events before (or since…)

This St. Mary's can be traced back to a chapel in Woburn erected by the last abbot of the Abbey in about 1535. It was damaged in a Civil War skirmish in 1645. Most of it was demolished in the 1860's in preparation to build a new church on the same site, but the area was found to be too small, so it was rebuilt as a mortuary chapel.

A lone motorcyclist and sidecar approaches while the Black Horse is having its windows cleaned on this unused card c.1955. The trees to the old church frontage are still there.

A very Gothic-inspired view of the old and new St Mary's from the 1898 book "Our Own Country".

The tower used to be shorter, but architect Edward Blore drew up plans and it was raised in 1829 and 1830. Blore also added a passage between the church and the tower, beautified the chancel and designed a new east window which was filled with stained glass. Six new bells were supplied by Thomas Mears of Whitechapel and a new clock was installed in 1830.

The building you see today was actually re-erected after being demolished in the 1860's, but the tower is original.

THE MORTUARY CHAPEL AND NEW CHURCH, WOBURN.

In 1981 it was declared redundant and it now houses the Woburn Heritage Centre.

Bedford Street, Woburn.

The most northernly postcard I have of Bedford Street is this 1916-used card, showing the Phipps' public house the Magpie. To the left, at nos.19 & 20, stood Woburn's first Workhouse, built in 1734. It was closed and sold in 1837 after the Poor Law came in.

WOBURN - WEST TO EAST

Alfred Dawborn (1820-1919) at the front of Birdcatcher's Cottage on Leighton Street. He made a living by trapping birds to sell to wealthy ladies as colourful songbirds. It is said he dipped common sparrows in yellow dye to make them more saleable!

A long empty road out of Woburn to the west along Leighton Street. Maryland, originally the Duchess of Bedford's Cottage Hospital, is off to the right. The card is titled, very faintly, 'Pinfold Pond' and was made by Cheetham, the photographer of Woburn Sands, who embossed his cards with his name, left.

A third Cheetham embossed card, showing the front of Maryland. Built in 1903 by Duchess Mary, after being her cottage hospital it became Bedfordshire's Residential College for Adult Education in 1967, under Principal Brian Cairns. Some of his expert sketches of Woburn featured on postcards themselves. Unsent.

A view along Leighton Street with Maryland in (almost) splendid isolation. Sent to Miss Louie Jones at the hospital pictured, the writers, "Both at no.29" apologised for not going to see her, but their maid was away ill and they had lots of visitors. The building, right, was Woburn's first police station, built in 1848. Card used in 1913.

Meal Times
Breakfast— 8.30 a.m.
(Sunday 9.00 a.m.)
Coffee— 11.00 a.m.
Lunch— 1.00 p.m.
Tea— 4.00 p.m.
Dinner— 7.00 p.m.
(Friday 7.15 p.m.)
Maryland has a bar.

Bedrooms
While there are some single rooms, most of the accommodation is in double rooms.

Facilities
There is a telephone call box for the use of students —the number is Woburn 634.

There is a Car Park for the use of students.

Soap and shoe-cleaning materials are provided.

Please bring your towel.

Booking a course
Bookings should be sent to the Principal, enclosing the course fee; cheques etc. being payable to Bedfordshire County Council.

All correspondence to:
The Principal, Maryland, Woburn, Bletchley, Bucks.

From a prospectus of courses run at Maryland in the summer of 1971. These included Reading to Learn, Bird Study, Antique Silver & Glass, Bedfordshire History, Landscape Painting and Italian Language. Residential prices were £12-15 a course.

The Round House, or Windmill Cottage as it was once known. It is still situated behind Birdcatcher's Cottage and Maryland. It was the base of a smock windmill, first mentioned in the 1660s, until converted into a cottage between 1805 and 1820 for John, 6th Duke of Bedford.

The Order of Service from January 26th, 1919, held in Woburn Church. As well as the local men who died, Dame Mary Russell, Duchess of Bedford, converted part of Woburn Abbey into a military hospital during World War One and some evacuated soldiers also died there.

A tablet in the church was erected to the 16 men who died in the Woburn Military Hospital 1914-1920 and also in memory of South African Johannes Zacherias Truter F.R.C.S. Edin., the Assistant Surgeon of the hospital who died at Woburn Abbey on 15th December 1918.

Congregation sitting.

Organ Voluntary.

THE MEMORIAL SERVICE.

Congregation standing.

In memory of 41 men of the Parish of Woburn who have given their lives fighting for their Country and for their homes in the Great War of 1914-1918.

Thomas Adamson	Herbert Mitchell
Horace Andrews	Albert Murrer
Raymond Andrews	John Newbury
Walter Birch	William Newbury
Ernest Bodsworth	George Peacock
Caleb Britchford	Arthur Phillips
William Burnage	Jack Phillips
Frederick Champkin	Fred Pickering
Charles Clarke	Harry Prestidge
William Coleman	Christopher Robinson
William Cook	Percy Skinner
George Drew	Wilfrid Skinner
Alec Emery	Cyril Smith
George Gilks	Milford Smith
William Gilks	Walter Stanford
Lionel Hammond	Francis Stanford
Bert Indge	David Sturgeon
Edward Kirk	Baron Tanqueray
William Kinna	Thomas Wilkinson
Harry Lewis	George Yole
Charles Ludgate	

Greater love hath no man than this, that a man lay down his life for his friends.

—St. John xv., verse 13.

A house in Bloomsbury Close, off London End, looking newly built when this was posted in June 1908. This area had been the site of the second Woburn Workhouse, which was closed and sold in 1898.

Looking towards the crossroads and the back of the Town Hall. The cottages on the right are fairly typical Bedford Estates, built for the agricultural workers. In 1925, rent was 2/6 per week, comprising a living room, kitchen, scullery, three bedrooms with coal barn and W.C. outside; gas lighting, mains drainage and water.

Closer to the Town Hall now, Barclays Bank once used the building on the left but in 1914 it was only open on Monday and Friday, from 2-4pm. Later remodelled, it was Annie's Bistro and is now a Thai Restaurant. Card unused.

Having crossed the road and entered Park Street, this is a view back towards the crossroads. All the sender's message is on this side, as the card pre-dates the divided back. Edie sent it to Miss Roberts in Luton in 1903. The church tower is just visible.

St. Mary's Church, Woburn.

A Gregory postcard view taken of the new St. Mary's church from the tower of the old one in c.1906. After the demolition of the old St. Mary's, the site was found to be too small to erect the new church as planned, so a new site was sought. The Duke provided land on Park Street where a pond had once been.

The church cost £25,000 and was consecrated on 23rd September 1868. Originally built with a spire, this was later found to be unsafe and had to be removed. This image is from a *carte d'visite* which must pre-date that change in 1892.

The design included a crypt beneath it and a trapdoor through which coffins could be lowered. It was originally intended to be the burial place of the Duke of Bedford and family, but they have continued to use their ancient mausoleum at Chenies in Bucks.

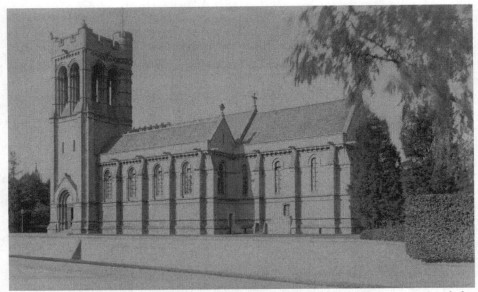

A Cheetham view of the church from Park Street. When built, it contained the heaviest bell in the county - 55 cwt., but the bells from both old and new churches were recast in 1910.

Interior views were difficult for early photographers. What they needed was an abundance of light, which churches often had. The elaborately carved Reredos behind the altar is by Kempe and was installed in the new St Mary's in 1903. It was commissioned by Adeline, widow of the 10th Duke, in his memory and was carved in Oberammergau.

This card was sent to Hilda Clues of Stockgrove Park by Bernie, in celebration of Hilda's birthday, June 1905.

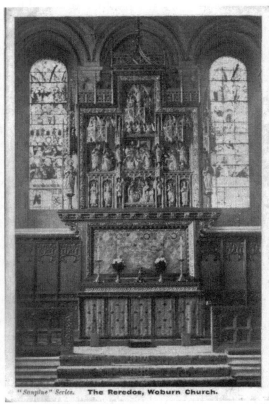

"Sunplus" Series. **The Reredos, Woburn Church.**

"Sandpine" Series. THE PARK ENTRANCE, WOBURN.

The entrance to Woburn Estate that most people will know - The Lion Lodge on Park Street. This was sent in December 1905. The road through the park was once private but is now classified as a 'C' road.

A mother (or perhaps a nursery nurse) out with a baby in a pram at the same spot, posted on Christmas Eve 1907 from Wolverton to Tamworth. A gardener, resting on his spade for a moment, has been caught just behind her.

A lone working man walking home after a long day? At least his route was picturesque. An unsent Cheetham postcard c.1908. The road through the park cuts between the Upper and Lower Drakeloe Ponds.

Park Farm Lodge, Woburn.

Once through the tree-lined landscaped gardens, you come to Park Farm Lodge. Away to the side, Park Farm was designed in 1795 by Robert Salmon for Francis, 5th Duke of Bedford. It now houses the Bedford Estate offices. Sent to Miss Page in April 1906 to show her the gates the writer had to go through to get to town.

Sanpine Series   The West Front, Woburn Abbey.

Across to the right of the road, you cannot see the Abbey, but it stands about 1km away. Only three sides of the original building remain as the east wing was demolished in 1949-50. John Ian Robert Russell, 13th Duke of Bedford, opened the building to the public in 1955 to help pay his father's Death Duties. Unsent.

WOBURN ABBEY, FROM   THE LAKE.

John Russell, 4th Duke of Bedford, (1710-1771) was the First Lord of the Admiralty from 1744-48 and it is said he had a full-size ship built on the lake in front of the house where he could conduct official business whilst 'afloat'! Postcard unsent.

31

Stump Cross Avenue, Woburn

Stump Cross, the turning to enter the Safari Park now. It first opened in 1970 as a partnership by the 13th Duke and Chipperfield's. The notion of "driving through" live zoo exhibits was a novelty that attracted hundreds of thousands of visitors in the first year. The avenue eventually succumbed to Dutch elm disease.

Froxfield Park Lodge, Woburn.

Marking the eastern edge of the Park, the Froxfield Park Lodge keeper is waiting by his gate. Sent from East Street in Aspley Guise just to let the recipient know that the sender had indeed received a card from them earlier that day.

Just the other side of the gatehouse stands this house at Froxfield. Sent with best wishes from Gramps (the man pictured?) and Aunt Mary to family in Croydon on Christmas Eve 1909. The 1911 census shows John and Mary Jane Sprague as living at Froxfield, a father and daughter. If it were them, John was then 94 and Mary 61.

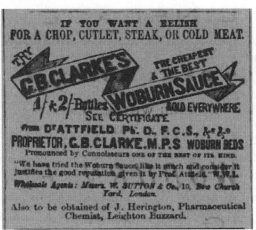

George Bowdler Clarke, the Woburn chemist, was promoting a 'Woburn Sauce' in 1873. Herbs and spices were flooding into England's ports from all parts of the Empire, giving a new choice to consumers of hitherto unknown flavours. It might have rivalled HP Sauce, but the recipe for this meat accompaniment disappeared long ago.

Province of Bedfordshire.

Lovell's Bury Lodge, No. 4018.

W. BRO. F. E. HAMILTON, W.M.

Consecration Banquet

AT THE

BEDFORD ARMS HOTEL,

WOBURN,

20TH FEBRUARY, 1920.

An event at the Bedford Arms, in February 1920, to consecrate the new local Lodge of the Freemasons. The programme gives the menu, which consisted of Soup, Fish with Turbot & Lobster Sauce, Joints of Roast Beef & Leg of Mutton, Sweets of Mince Pies, Fruit Salad and Trifle, Cheese with Celery, Coffee and Dessert. Printed by Timaeus of Bedford.

WOBURN - OTHERS

Some cards are a mystery. A Cheetham card sent in 1909, it looks like a Dog Show? With a Bookie? The Recreation ground has an old railway carriage as a pavilion which I am told was at Woburn. Cheetham took more than one view of this event.

Unnamed groups on unposted cards are always sad to see, as no-one has a reason to keep them. However, this came from an album with other Woburn cards in and I think Alfred Dawborn, the Woburn bird catcher, is second from right at the back. He had seven sons and six daughters, so perhaps this is some of them.

Who died at Woburn, Jan. 23rd, 1876.

Carte d'visite of ordinary citizens are usually unnamed, unless the owner wrote their name on the reverse.

The extra information printed onto this example means this must be Ann Price, wife of John, an accountant. They lived on Park Street on the 1851 census, along with an 18-year-old visitor, Honoria Valentine. By the 1871 census, they had moved to Bedford Street. Ann died aged 63.

"A funeral was conducted on Friday week by Mr. Harbert, with his new funeral car. This was one of the quietest and best-conducted funerals we ever remember to have seen." (Luton Times, February 1876)

The card was made by photographer Mr. Turner of Barnsbury, London.

Two early *carte d'visite* from Woburn photographers, Daniels and Clarke, with their backstamps. I am not sure when smiling for portraits became the norm, but obviously not by the 1880s-1890s…

These duplicated images produced a 3D effect when used with a stereoscopic viewer. Sadly, there are no details of who those pictured are, posing with a horse at the "Porter's Lodge, Woburn Abbey".

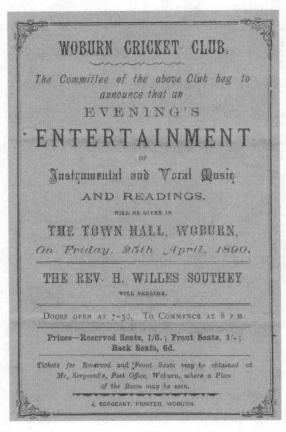

WOBURN CRICKET CLUB.

The Committee of the above Club beg to
announce that an

EVENING'S

ENTERTAINMENT

OF

Instrumental and Vocal Music

AND READINGS,

WILL BE GIVEN IN

THE TOWN HALL, WOBURN,

On Friday, 25th April, 1890.

THE REV. H. WILLES SOUTHEY

WILL PRESIDE.

DOORS OPEN AT 7-30. TO COMMENCE AT 8 P.M.

Prices—Reserved Seats, 1/6.; Front Seats, 1/-;
Back Seats, 6d.

Tickets for Reserved and Front Seats may be obtained at
Mr. Serjeant's, Post Office, Woburn, where a Plan
of the Room may be seen.

J. SERJEANT, PRINTER, WOBURN.

Members of the families of Andrews, Gilby, Tompkins and Negus, all Woburn trades-people, were taking part in this event. There were Pianoforte duets, violin solos and recitations.

Cricket was very popular in Woburn as several of the Dukes and wider Russell family were keen on the game. John Russell, 4th Duke of Bedford, had set up a local team by 1743 which competed at a high level. Lord Charles Russell, sixth son of the 6th Duke, wrote a book of his recollections of Lord's and Bedfordshire cricket in 1879, published by the Woburn printer Fisher. Lord Charles had played first-class cricket for the Marylebone Cricket Club between 1833 and 1846.

This private photo taken by a roving inn-sign photographer shows the signboard of the Magpie at 18 Bedford Street in the mid-1960s(?). It is now run under the name of Long's Hotel, as a William Long ran an inn called the Woolsack here, in the 1650s.

Bedfordshire Archives has a list 48 Woburn premises once used as inns, as well as the Fowler Brothers brewery, based at the Birchmoor Arms for a time, before Henry Fowler ended up in the Bedford Lunatic Asylum.

PHIPPS' HOUSE

PHIPPS' HOUSE

THE MAGPIE

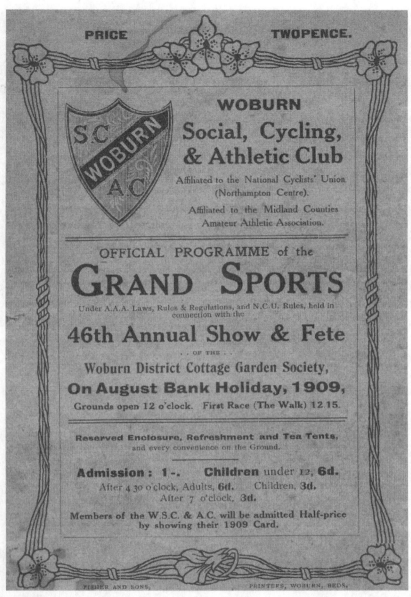

PRICE TWOPENCE.

WOBURN
Social, Cycling, & Athletic Club

Affiliated to the National Cyclists' Union
(Northampton Centre).

Affiliated to the Midland Counties
Amateur Athletic Association.

OFFICIAL PROGRAMME of the

GRAND SPORTS

Under A.A.A. Laws, Rules & Regulations, and N.C.U. Rules, held in
connection with the

46th Annual Show & Fete

. . OF THE . .

Woburn District Cottage Garden Society,

On August Bank Holiday, 1909,

Grounds open 12 o'clock.   First Race (The Walk) 12.15.

Reserved Enclosure, Refreshment and Tea Tents,
and every convenience on the Ground.

Admission : 1 -.   Children under 12, **6d.**
After 4 30 o'clock, Adults, **6d.**   Children, **3d.**
After 7 o'clock, **3d.**

Members of the W.S.C. & A.C. will be admitted Half-price
by showing their 1909 Card.

FISHER AND SONS,   PRINTERS, WOBURN, BEDS.

Another Fisher production; the Grand Woburn Sports Day programme in 1909. Walking races were very popular, especially in Woburn. The son of Mr. Hammond (who had the Bedford Arms for a time before moving to the Swan at Woburn Sands), had broken a World Record the previous year, walking 131 miles & 580 yards in 24 hours. There was a 20-mile walk at this event, with Oxo vehicles on the route to refresh the entrants! The Luton Red Cross Silver Prize Band were on hand to entertain the crowds. Sadly, it rained on the day and the event made a loss.

To finish Woburn, a few aerial views from the old St. Mary's tower. Looking towards the north, the tallest building in the centre is the Magpie. To the extreme left is the Bell, another historic Woburn inn. Away in the distance is Crawley Road and fields now under Eleanor and Drakeloe Closes. Sent to Wandsworth in 1915.

Possibly taken at the same time as the last, a view east, with a lady and pram just passing the door of no.11 Bedford Street. This is one of the oldest properties in Woburn, believed to be 16th century in parts.

Looking south from the tower, this shows the back of the Market Place buildings. The row of barns running off the Market Place (centre to right) are still there. The chapel building, centre, is the Congregationalist Chapel, demolished in 1988. Sent by Ethel with belated birthday greetings to her friend Edith Anstee at Cranfield Mill.

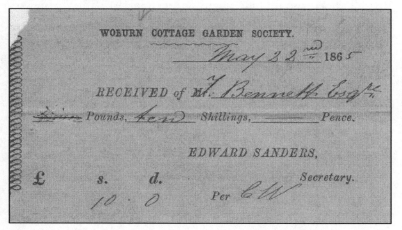

A receipt for Mr. Bennett's subscription to the Woburn Cottage Garden Society, 1865. The society covered not only Woburn, but places as far away as Cranfield, Great Brickhill and Fenny Stratford. Their annual show was a highlight of the social calendar.

A rare view of inside the Town Hall when it was fitted out with a snooker table and card room. This comes from an ornate presentation book given to Rev. Charles Russell Dickinson on his leaving Woburn in 1912 after being vicar there for 12 years.

ASPLEY GUISE - THE SQUARE

Like Woburn, many of the cards of Aspley Guise feature the centre where roads meet; views most people would recognise. The Courtney Memorial Hall is on the left and Church Street rises in the background. Crute's grocery and provision shop looks well stocked. The shop to the right is P. E Balderston, another fruiterer and greengrocers. Sent from Ma & Pa to Mrs. Lucas, Northampton, 1928.

Another view into Church Street, sent a little earlier in 1913. Two different shopkeepers had their trades here then. Day & Co., grocers, while J. W. Goodall advertises "Boots, Shoes & General Store" on his shopboard, yet he appears as a baker, confectioner and corn dealer in trade directories?

A view into West Hill, here called Station Road. The wagon belongs to Harry Barker, a carrier, of Woburn Sands. He ferried goods between Woburn Sands and Bedford. The sign for the Steamer beerhouse can just be made out in the background. The posters on the lamp noticeboard are for joining the Army Reserve. Sent in 1920 by Edi, who was staying at the Bell, just behind the cameraman to the left.

This view of the other side of the Square can be dated to July 1916 by the newspaper boards outside John Warrick's tobacconist about a Zeppelin bombing raid. The card must have been sent in an envelope by Robert Ash (a relative of Herbert the grocer?) so there was no stamp or postmark.

Sent to show the sender was staying at the Holt. This was once the home of Francis Moore. A pupil at the Academy, he married the Head's daughter! He prospered and had the Holt built in 1786. It was modified and extended in the 19th century, becoming eventually becoming a hotel named after him.

A series of three cards showing front, back and gardens of the Holt / Moore Place Hotel. These were all produced and sold by E. Bathurst's Pharmaceutical Chemist in Woburn Sands. Sadly none are sent, but they can be dated c.1910-1914.

The Pagoda, left, was featured in sketches of the building in the 1850's. Francis Moore was responsible for planting most the woods seen around Aspley Guise and Woburn Sands. He realised the area was ideal for fast-growing trees, bought up the open heath land cheaply and planted more than 50,000 Scotch fir trees around 1778. When they matured, he sold them as timber. The *Royal Society for the Encouragement of Art and Manufactures & Commerce* even gave him a gold medal for doing so. He was not popular with the old-guard gentry of Aspley Guise though and had a long-running feud with the How family.

Moore sold his 500-acre woods to the Duke of Bedford in 1792 for more than £17,000, making a considerable profit. Both his son, John Patrick Moore and grandson, John Vaux Moore (who became Rector of Aspley), were both influential benefactors to the village and funded refurbishments to the church.

The following is an Account of the Planta-
tion of Scotch Firs, for which the Gold
Medal was adjudged to Francis Moore,
of Aspley Guise, Esq. in the Year 1779.

To the Society for the Encouragement of
Arts, Manufactures, and Commerce.

Gentlemen,

THE perusal of your annual book, wherein you offer premiums, induced me to become a candidate for your favour, and humbly to submit the following account of Plantations of Scotch Firs, and the consequent improvement of barren (and otherwise useless) land, to your attention.

I live in a part of England, about forty miles distant from London, where some of the land is exceedingly sandy, poor, and mountainous, and totally unfit for cultivation, at least the expence of cultivating

     I   it

Part of Moore's letter to the Society explaining his planting project. He goes on to say that he could expect 676 trees per acre to mature *"...which at the age of twenty-six years may be fairly computed to be of the value of 1s. 6d. per tree or nett profit £50 17s per acre."*

It was Moore's planting that gave Aspley and surrounding area the reputation as a health resort with medicinal airs in the latter half of the 19th century.

Moore had his home built on the Square in 1786 on land that had belonged to his father-in-law, the Rev. Robert Sawell, ex-Head of Aspley Academy c.1734-1770.

THE HOLT, ASPLEY GUISE

That Pagoda again, sent in July 1916. Eva writes to her friend Dolly Sell in Cheam: *"Fred's brother Jesse who was killed used to be the gardener at this house, it faces our house."* Presumably this was Pte. William Jesse Maynard, 5th Bn., Beds. Regt., who died of wounds on 13th September 1915, aged just 20.

THE SQUARE. ASPLEY GUISE.

An early undivided-back card published by Herbert Gregory. He had worked locally for Powage Press before setting up his own small works in Woburn Sands. The writer chose to barely use the message panel. Sent to Wealdstone on May 31st 1903.

Not all cards are Edwardian - this one from the mid-1960s shows a Post Office business in the Square. No shops remain at all now…

Among the few notable events in the Square, this is the Duke of Bedford opening a Memorial Drinking Trough to honour the late Emma Courtney. According to the message, *"The Lady with the one feather on her hat and & shade is the Duchess. The Duke is standing next to her wearing a straw hat. We are in the crowd, but too small, I suppose, to be seen".* The ivy has since been removed from the houses behind.

Goodall's bakery is next door to the Anchor here; he must have moved premises onto the Square later. The two errand boys are beaming at the camera, pleased to have been in the shot! An unused Cheetham postcard.

That corner shop was still a bakery in the early 1960s, the giant HOVIS sign outside is a clue. By now the shops on the Square were A. Bray and F. Tripp. Another outpost of the Dudeney & Johnston's chain of grocers stands off to the right.

A business card for the Master of Art at Aspley Academy, Augustin Georgerie. Apparently, he died in January 1805: *"A few days ago, in London, Mr. Georgery, drawing-master at Aspley academy, and late of this town."* (Northampton Mercury)

Bedford Road leaves the Square next to the Bell, where two customers have stepped out through the front door that you would dare not use today! There has been a Bell public house in Aspley since the 1780's, but there were then Upper and Lower Bell's. We do not know which this Bell was. An unused card from Holmes' Post Office.

A Church of England Mission card issued for a visit to Aspley Guise by Rev. Canon R. T. Whittendon, the rector of Orset in Essex.

It contains a short "Prayer for Perseverance" for the recipient to write-in what they were particularly resolving to do. This was the time of a great temperance movement to get men out of public houses and more sober.

There are 5 'Helps to Holiness' on the rear, but no.3, "*Always attend the Celebration of the Holy Communion every Sunday, and receive It at least once a month at an early service.*" has had the '*Always…*' replaced with '*Try to…*' and '*…if possible.*' added to the end, by hand!

Not a postcard, but a view that will not be seen again - the organ which was still inside the Courtney Memorial Hall until it ceased to function as a chapel.

Starting life as the British School, it only became a chapel when the other school in Woburn Lane became the Board School in 1879. The lady running this independent chapel and mission room was Miss Emma Courtney. She organised lectures, sermons and temperance events here until her death in 1906, aged 87. Her friends renamed the hall in her honour after her death.

Lastly of the Square, this view was used in 1918 and has a lady in a dark skirt, white blouse and hat stood prominently in shot. You will see her often in postcards further on. This is Miss Alice Holmes, who published these cards from her village Post Office.

HEALTH RESORT.

The Climate of Aspley Guise, Bedfordshire.

(ONE MILE FROM WOBURN SANDS STATION, L. & N.-W. Ry.)

Extract from a Work published by DR. WILLIAMS, of Malvern, on "The Topography & Climate of Aspley."

"SOME years ago, ill-health in Herefordshire induced me to seek a residence upon a dry soil. I was pleased to find ASPLEY GUISE, in Bedfordshire, was upon a deep green sand formation. I shall never forget the sensations I experienced in walking up the sandy lane from Woburn Sands Station to the Village. Here, thought I, is the spot I have long sighed for; and resolved to pitch my tent and seek that greatest of earthly blessings—HEALTH.

"The air of ASPLEY is generally admitted to be very pure, buoyant, and exhilarating. Its freshness, particularly in elevated situations, has been compared to a sea-breeze.

An extract taken from Dr. Williams' book extolling the virtues of Aspley Guise for your health. He compared the rainfall, air quality and temperatures to Nice, Madeira and Pau, concluding that Aspley Guise was much better! This extract was printed by Powage Press.

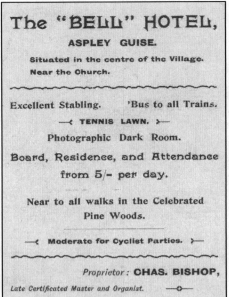

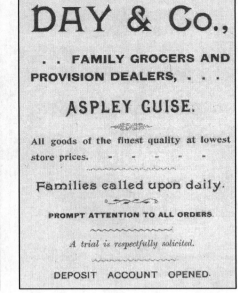

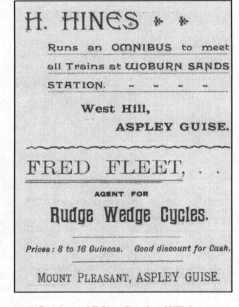

Some local adverts from Herbert Gregory's "*Guide and View Book of Woburn Sands, Aspley Guise and Woburn*", published in 1904. The book was republished and sold at a church fete in 1952 as a novelty.

ASPLEY GUISE - NORTH TO THE SQUARE

The Crossing, Aspley Guise

Here she is again at the railway station. The line opened in 1846, connecting Bedford with Bletchley and later Oxford to Cambridge before being truncated back to Bedford-Bletchley again. Aspley Guise was only a 'Halt' to start with, meaning no raised platforms and trains would not stop unless they knew they had to. Passengers had to climb down from the coaches.

Not a postcard, but too interesting not to use here; this is the inside of the crossing-keepers hut at Aspley Guise station, on a press photograph from the Echo & Post in 1976. Somewhere railway staff could sit in the warm and dry between trains.

Salford Road, Aspley Guise.

7.

Here, Miss Holmes is taking to the residents of nos.102-104 Salford Road. In her time of running both Woburn Sands and later Aspley Guise Post Offices, she produced a huge range of cards. Nearly 90 have been identified, the earliest used in 1916.

A needlework sampler worked by Ellen Saunders at the British School, Aspley Guise (later Courtney Hall) in 1852 to show her skills:

"Time by moments steals away,
First the hour and then the day,
Small the daily loss appears,
Yet it soon amounts to years."

How very true! According to the 1851 census, Ellen was 10 when she made this. Her father was a shoemaker in East Street (Bedford Road).

57

As we travel towards the Square, we reach St. Botolph's. The Victorian-look belies its 800–900-year history. It houses a tomb of a knight, thought to be Sir William de Tyrynton, who may have died c.1400 and two floor brasses, presumed to be John Danvers, Rector 1395-1414 and Sir John de Gyse IV of about 1500.

A writer, J. D. Parry, lamented in 1845 of the church (before it was extended) *"The church was certainly much too small for the increased population of the parish, amounting to 1100… a very considerable portion, nearly all the gallery, was occupied by the inmates of a boarding school in the village."*

A man is sweeping-up in the lychgate. Although the postmark date is obscured, it's probably First World War as the sender says they are going to Crawley Crossing to see the home troop trains, as the stations "here" are closed and only for soldiers.

The Lady Chapel (15th Century Screen) St Botolph's, Aspley Guise   75.

The tomb thought to be of knight Sir William de Tyrynton can be seen in this view inside the church. Much work has been done to the building over the centuries, including the head of Aspley Guise Classical Academy, William

14th Century Font, St Botolphs Aspley Guise 73

Wright, providing a gallery to west end for his own and his school's use in 1799. Undated Holmes card. The 14th century font on an unused Holmes card.

The main restoration of the building was carried out by Rev. John Vaux Moore in 1844 at his own expense. This grandson of Francis Moore (the tree planter) was Rector here from 1844 until his death in 1864. The restoration included rebuilding the chancel, much of the nave and the north aisle. Not everyone approved: *"The preservation of the miserable organ, and the gallery, is to be regretted: light, which is much wanted in this part of the church, is consequently excluded by this trumpery erection. A little contrivance, without losing space, would have placed the font in its proper position…"*, complained John Martin, librarian to the Duke of Bedford.

Another stereo view by photographer Daniels of Tingrith and Woburn. Note the dreaded APSLEY misspelling! Rev. John Vaux Moore paid for a complete set of new stained-glass windows for the church.

Church towers usually afford good views and Aspley's is no exception. This one shows a building now known as the Old Rectory (used 1869-1919), beside the church to the south. In the hazy distance the Mount Pleasant area can just be made out. Used in 1933.

Hove is a long way from Bedfordshire! I wonder if Thomas Wiles came this far for business, or was he just here on holiday with his camera and saw an opportunity? He produced 100s of cards of his home area. The thatched house, east of the church, was once the stables for the Rectory. Used in 1920.

View from Church Tower, Aspley Guise.

Miss Holmes produced views from the tower too, this is undated but c.1920s. Part of the wall around Aspley House gardens is on the left and the side of the house known as the Shrubbery is on the right.

THE AVENUE.
"A PRETTY WALK" ASPLEY GUISE, BEDFORDSHIRE

The Avenue is off Church Street. Several large houses are there now, but once the main house was the home of the How's, an old Quaker family synonymous with Aspley Guise for 200 years, having also lived at the Old House.

Aspley Guise was assessed under the Rating & Valuation Act in 1927. Avenue House was then owned and occupied by Dr. John Gregory White, a relative of the How's. The valuer commented: *"Was old Cottage 300 years old. Only 3 beds with fireplaces. Miss Orlebar had it at £45 rent. Present owner has added a Bath room. Says he thinks worth £65. Old house in lovely spot with good garden"*.

This view was taken c.1920. Sadly, we only have a picture of the drive.

The garden wall of Aspley House runs along Church Street. The Old House was built around 1575 for Edmund Harding, eventually being sold to the Cartwright family whose heiress married into the How family.

Aspley House, next door, was built about 1690 for William Norcliffe on the site of an earlier structure and was reworked in the 1740s. The last of the Norcliffe's moved to Bedford where they died in 1762 and the house was sold to James Reynolds of Clerkenwell. Rev. Hervey of Hulcote bought the house at the end of 1786 and it remained in their family possession until 1939.

Opposite the wall, the Shrubbery was once a beerhouse called the Swan (c.1822-c.1851) before the name was transferred to another house on Bedford Road. Apparently, the inn was close to the Church and therefore handy for Vestry meetings rather than use the cold draughty church.

The next view along this road shows the Powage Press. The printer was a significant employer for the village. John Kemp bought the former buildings of the Aspley Guise Classical Academy in 1874. On 12th December 1911, the business burnt to the ground but was swiftly rebuilt. Unsent card.

The view from the reverse. Aspley Academy was said to have rivalled Eton in the 18th century, attracting the sons of rich tradesmen from far and wide. There is a mural monument to the memory of Headmaster William Wright in the church. Unsent Holmes postcard.

The chain fence visible in the last forms part of the frontage of Chain House, left. A cottage, "Brown's Hovel", once stood between it and the Anchor Inn. In 1925 Chain House was two dwellings. The chains were removed in World War II for the scrap metal drive…

...as can be seen on a card sent in 1959. It was later a bed and breakfast business under Mr. & Mrs. Jeffery. It was built as a house for the schoolmaster of the Academy. It was listed in 1961, which considered it to be late 18th century *"probably a refronting of an earlier building"*.

Good accomodation for Cyclists & Motorists. Luncheons & Teas provided. Ales, Wines & Spirits of the best quality. 5 mins. from Motor-trains (ASPLEY GUISE), 1 mile from Woburn Sands. Situated in the midst of the celebrated Woburn Pine Woods.
Usher, Woburn Sands, Photo.   W. COOPEY, Proprietor, Aspley Guise.

The Anchor is still in business today, the name first appearing at the Woburn Petty Sessions in the late 1850's. It was then in the hands of a Dennis Wooding. He was reported for fighting with James Burton, the licensee of the Bell across the Square, in 1856! This card is unsent, but Coopey was landlord there from 1905-23.

The First World War interrupted tranquil village life and naval reservist Coopey was called up. He received his official orders in August 1914 but returned six weeks later as his eyesight was found to be impaired. (Beds Times 7th Aug. & 30th Oct.). He was to be often found dressed as a minstrel, playing his banjo for local children and throwing pennies for them to chase. After the war, Coopey suffered from depression and in February 1923, he took his own life, aged 66 years old. He had gone out to one of the outbuildings to bring in some coal but did not return. He was found by his wife with his throat cut.

The buildings opposite the Anchor. The three-storey building was once the Aspley Guise Post Office under John Shemeld in 1869. Those nearer the camera were those of the local smithy and cart repairer Richard Walters. This is numbered No.1 of the Holmes postcard series.

Aspley Guise Village

Valentines Series

And so we reach the Square again. A version of this view was sent in July 1921. The edge of Goodall's bakery sign is on the left. The Bell is the middle left, the Holt middle right. The house with bay window, right, has gone completely now.

ASPLEY GUISE - EAST TO THE SQUARE

East of Aspley Guise Square, south off the Bedford Road, is modern Mount Pleasant. The area grew up to accommodate traders and business families who could afford to live away from the poorer and more cramped centre of the village. The junction off Bedford Road was then more of a fork, with this right-hand way having more importance than the left-hand way on to Church End of Husborne Crawley.

Coming back towards Bedford Road, this row of cottages is on the left, now nos.84-86 Mount Pleasant. Seen here is the grocer's shop in the hands of Thomas William Crute. Lipton's Tea, Colman's Starch and Mustard and Home & Colonial Tea would have been good sellers in 1910 when this was posted.

Thomas Crute and his mother (and cats) stand in front of the first cottage on the left of the last picture. His father, Fred, was a bricklayer for Woburn Abbey, who died in 1932 aged 83.

After a £1 note went missing from Crute's shop in 1925, he laid a trap by marking some 10s. notes and waiting for one to be stolen. It was duly found to have been removed by one of his workers. He got probation for two years and was fined 22s. 6d. This view up back towards the main road is undated, but c.1905.

The same bend, from the reverse, on a Holmes card. In the 1850s, only the very top of Mount Pleasant, near the Gypsy Lane turn, used that name; the lower part up to the Wheatsheaf was just known as part of East Street, as Bedford Road was then known. The area between the two was known as New Town.

Looking up the road, with Miss Holmes present, just above the San Remo Road turn. Cottages sprang up here during the 1800's with space for gardens and better sanitation as most houses here had their own well. The name San Remo had appeared by 1915, but I do not know why this exotic name was used.

San Remo Road was a later addition by residential speculators on land that was once Mr. Handscomb's nursery. Miss Holmes on a card sent to Miss Dickens, of 2 Leon Cottages, Bletchley with best Christmas wishes and news that "F." had now started work this week, good news in a Depression, in December 1931.

This is the Wheatsheaf Inn that the Britten family ran from 1841 to 1900, with female landladies for 36 of those years. In 1900 it was sold to Jarvis, brewers of Bedford, who were then bought out by Charles Wells Ltd. in 1917.

Before Wells took over, Jarvis tore down the old building in 1906 and erected a modern one. After serving local residents for more than 170 years (including under Bill & Ann Cox, 1978-2004) it was closed in 2011 and demolished in 2013 to be residential properties. The Barnwell family butchers shop stood opposite.

"Sandylands" is now known as Peacehaven on Spinney Lane. Bought by the West family in 1924, they hosted many events to aid Barnardo's Homes. Their own son escaped Singapore in 1942 with 11 others in a rowing boat. The West's left in 1953. This view is from Spinney Lane, outside the modern Lower School.

The cottages that originally stood by the turn for Spinney Lane were cleared away and smart new Council were properties built. Aspley Guise Council raised an issue with Ampthill Rural District Council in 1927 that they only had six such properties and needed many more.

As the plaque states, the Methodist Chapel was opened in 1813. It was later renewed and repaired in 1881 by Mr. Poole of Woburn Sands at a cost of £93 13s. and a new American organ was installed in 1889.

"An interesting and pretty wedding was witnessed at the Wesleyan Chapel, Aspley Guise, on Saturday, when Mr James Cooper's only daughter, Annie Elizabeth, was married to Mr T. B. Dicken, who has lately returned from India. The bride is well-known in Salford, having for some years been a pupil teacher in its School when Miss Saxby was the Mistress; and, for her wedding, she was tastefully attired in a costume of cream cloth, with a hat to match. Arthur Cooper acted as the bridegroom's best man. The service was conducted by the Rev. E. Reverley, and Miss Chappell presided at the organ. Afterwards, a reception was held at the home of the bride's aunt, Mrs T. Rich, at Mount Pleasant. The happy pair received many costly and useful presents." (Beds. Mercury, January 1909)

This came to me with "*Aspley Guise Chapel*" hand-written on the rear, but as it closed in 1978 and is now a private house, I have been unable to confirm this. This is too small to be the main room, but it may have been a side room?

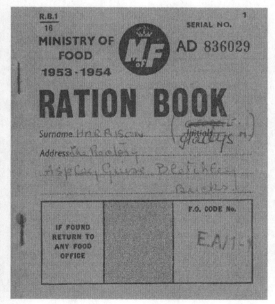

The ration book for Gladys Harrison of the Rectory, Aspley Guise. Some of the pages within are stamped by the shops of A. Bray and W. Bailey.

Rationing did not end when the Second World War did, some items continued to be hard to get. Fourteen years of food rationing in Britain finally ended at midnight on 4th July 1954, when the last restrictions on the sale and purchase of meat and bacon were lifted.

A Bathurst's Pharmacy view of the backs of the houses in Mount Pleasant. Undated, but c.1910. Benjamin Wiffen lived at the Haven, the last house on the eastern side by the Gypsy Lane crossroads, after he retired from his ironmongery in Woburn.

We are now down at the junction with Bedford Road. This house stood on the western side of the turn, but was demolished post-Second World War. The road here has been slightly re-aligned, as it used to pass on the other side of the grassed area where the timber bus shelter now stands. A Holmes card used in 1933.

A rare case of a road moving away from a house! Park Cottage survives and now has some space between it and the modern road. Bedford Road gradually assumed more importance than Mount Pleasant, especially after the coming of the M1.

On Bedford Road stands the Aspley Guise War Memorial, opened in April 1922. The names of 33 First World War casualties are remembered here and seven from the Second. The land it sits on was given by Aspley House, as both sons of the family in residence at that time died very early in the war; Lieut. Villiers Chernocke Downes, 1st Batt. Beds Regt., in October 1914, aged 23 and Second Lieut. Archer Chernocke Downes, 2nd Batt., Cheshire Regt., in November 1914, aged 22. Both were educated at the Knoll, Aspley Heath.

The wooden structure has been periodically replaced. The garden behind is now fenced off.

The Grade II* listing for this house says it was built about 1690 for William Norcliffe on the site of an earlier structure, reworked in the 1740s. William married the widowed daughter of the vicar of Aspley at that time. A later owner bought up the cottages behind the house and had them demolished.

ASPLEY HOUSE ABOUT 1820

A modern (if slightly stained) card of an old etching of the house. The Downes, mentioned previously, had rented it since 1891. Lt-Col. Charles Villiers Somerville Downes died there in 1909, aged 62. His widow, Catherine, stayed at the house until her death in 1938. She paid for the whole of the War Memorial's expenses.

Almost back to the Square again. An unused Gregory's card, but Sinfield House is X'ed to show something important. The Bell is centre left. The building with flagpole and white signboard on the front is another beerhouse, the Swan, opened after the earlier one on Church Street had closed.

Looking back towards Bedford in 1916. The Swan was closed down in 1909, but John Hines, the last landlord there, continued to run his cab business from the house.

The shop next door was an agent for Wellsbach incandescent lights and Swift Cycles here in 1905, but regretfully no signboard can be seen. Posted from Buxton back to Aspley. The writer, David, said he was just popping out to Camera Club.

The tightness of the road here has led to much modern traffic chaos; it looks much quieter here. Hard to date, but Benskins lasted until bought out by Ind Coope in 1957, but the Bell's sign may have lasted after that. It closed c.2000 and after being an Italian restaurant for a while, it is now the Blue Orchid Thai.

ASPLEY GUISE - SOUTH TO THE SQUARE

The parish boundary of Aspley Guise runs along Aspley Lane, just the other side of the Lodge shown here at the entrance to Birchmoor Farm. Therefore, the photographer and Lodge are in Woburn but the fields and woods in the background are in Aspley. Designed by H. Percy Adams, F.R.I.B.A., a sketch of the Lodge appeared in *Academy Architecture* in November 1910. Locally, Adams was also responsible for the South wing of Bedford General Hospital, Bedford County Hospital and Rignall Wood in Great Missenden. A Cheetham postcard used in 1916.

The trackway which leads off opposite the Lodge travelled in almost a straight line directly to the Henry VII Lodge, on the outskirts of Woburn Sands. Much of the path has been reinstated after the fuller's earth quarry extraction.

Further along Aspley Lane is the Birchmoor Pumping Station. A rare interior view of the building and the 50 h.p. gas pump that supplied water to the villages around. Messrs. Balfour & Sons advised sinking a well here in 1903. They thought a six-inch bore hole would cost £40 if drilled to eighty feet. Unsent.

This house stands on Woodside, between Wood Lane and Aspley Lane. Private household cards like this were likely made for the householder to send to their friends at Christmas etc. This is now known as Old Wood Place.

Peers Drive, now a cul-de-sac off Woburn Lane, was once the site of a large mansion. Built by Sinfield's before the First World War, Col. Frank Joseph Agabeg I.D.F., V.D., C.B.E., husband of Florence and father of Sybil Hoare and Enid Peers Agabeg, died there in 1927, aged 66.

In 1933, when home to Sir John and Lady Salt, it burnt down. Their three children, asleep in the house at the time, were safely rescued, as was much of the furnishings and valuables on the ground floor. Plans to rebuild it were later abandoned.

Built c.1900, this was demolished c.2007. An eclectic sale took place there in 1940, for Mr. Bannatyne, who was leaving: *"A 1935 Austin Saloon; 2 boarded buildings, carpenter's bench and tools; garden roller, wire netting. 3 garden frames and light; 16m. 1935 J.P motor mower; 21 hens (1938/9 hatched); 4 poultry houses: 9 bottles of Irish Whisky; and outdoor effects."*

The old National (Church of England) School was built in 1848. An 1850 report of this school said *"The master is a very respectable and conscientious man. I also think well of the intelligence and industry of the mistress"*, but *"the teaching in the boys' school is too mechanical."*

The Parish Hall was opened in December 1902 by Chas. Sinfield. The Duke gave £700 (and also opened it), Mr. Dymond £260, Mr. Harris (who died before completion) £250 and the other £420 was raised by villagers. A bazaar raised another £150 to fit it out. Before this, the British school in the Square was used for events.

John William Goodall operated as a baker and corn-dealer in Aspley Guise from at least 1890, according to Kelly's trade directories. The Leighton Buzzard Observer reported in August 1897:

"Aspley Guise. Local Success. Mr. J. W. Goodall, refreshment contractor, has gained certificate for excellence of quality in bread in connection with a competition organised by the Master Bakers' and Confectioners' Society."

By the next year, "Confectioner" had been added to his entry in Kelly's. In 1910, "Corn-dealer and Confectioner" were dropped from his entry, leaving just "Baker". The 1914 Kelly's was the last one he was listed in.

He was noted in many newspaper reports as having arranged the catering at local outdoor events. He was also Chairman of the Parish Council for some time and held a number of other local public offices. He was twice married and died in 1933.

Such parties always needed ginger beer, and Goodall made sure his bottles came back to him by purchasing ones with his name inscribed into them.

ASPLEY GUISE - WEST TO THE SQUARE

Aspley Hill, Woburn Sands

Aspley Guise parish starts at the bottom of the hill, but there are very few postcards of that as it was once a very poor area of crowded housing. The view from the top of Aspley Hill has been taken many times, as here with Miss Holmes. Woburn Sands sits at the bottom of the hill with Aspley Heath rising in the background. Aspley Heath was once part of Aspley Guise before becoming its own parish.

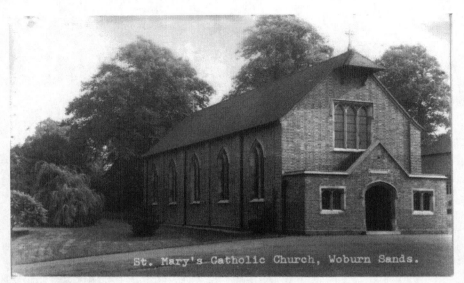

St. Mary's Catholic Church, Woburn Sands.

St. Mary's Catholic Church was consecrated in 1957 after earlier temporary premises had been used in Wood Street, Woburn Sands and Church Road, Aspley Heath. They also used the block opposite the Fir Tree Hotel when it was a hall, before conversion to hotel bedrooms. Unused card, c.1960s.

ST. MARY'S CATHOLIC CHURCH, WOBURN SANDS

It was funded by a bequest from Christine Chichester. St. Mary's was designed by John Comper, FRIBA, who had already worked on St. Gregory's at Northampton. A parishioner and local builder later offered to build a hall in the grounds, which was then named after his mother-in-law who had recently died. Unsent.

Looking down towards Woburn Sands from approximately where St. Mary's now stands. The outline of Edgbury in Aspley Heath is just visible on the horizon, left. Aspley Hill runs between the field and the houses.

An unknown mother and children, no doubt in their "Sunday-best" were captured on this grainy *carte d'visite* by H. Clarke, an Aspley Guise photographer c.1880s, who had worked for the Duke. The girl, right, clutches her doll.

Sadly faded, this unposted view shows the rear of houses in Weathercock Lane, with No.19 Littlebury nearest the camera. The three pairs of houses after the corner of Russell Street, nos.30-40 Weathercock Lane, are on the right, in the distance.

This view across the Aspley Guise and Woburn Sands Golf Club (which opened its first 9-holes in 1913) is the closest Miss Holmes gets to the lens on one of her cards! The rear of some Weathercock Lane properties are in the background.

This rule book was produced between 1920-1924. The entrance fee was 1 guinea, then 4 guineas a year for men and 3 for women. A Life Membership was available for £30. Residents of the immediate villages were not allowed to join as Temporary Members, nor to come in as Guests.

A caddie could be booked for 6d. for 9-holes or 1s. for 18, but players were warned not to buy balls from their Caddie, who would face instant dismissal and the Member expelled!

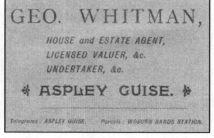

Some of the adverts from the Parish magazine of 1903. This had been relaunched at the start of the year, joining with other six other parishes to publish the "Fleete Ruridecanal Magazine". Mr. Whitman was obviously a man of many talents!

"Station Road", but this is the West Hill junction with Weathercock Lane, left and Woodside, right. A rare Holmes card that she didn't appear in. The buyer used it to record that they had stayed in Aspley at the Rookery twice in 1946.

Not a postcard, but a press photo of Radlett House, with Jack MacGougan, General Secretary of the National Union of Tailors & Garment Workers 1969-1979, no doubt visiting as the building was once used by ACAS as a venue for their conciliatory dispute resolution services.

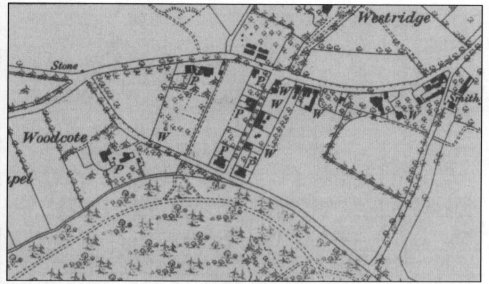

Part of the O.S. map of Bedfordshire (XXIV.NE). The Aspley Hill area was surveyed in 1881 and the results published in 1884. Very little had been built by this time, but a rush of genteel Victorian and Edwardians soon changed that.

West Hill House still stands on the west side of West Hill and Dukes Street. It was home to the Brigden family for 40 years. Strangely, I have never seen a card of the Duke's Head beerhouse, which operated opposite from c.1871-1953.

Duke Street was only laid out in 1869. This card was sent in 1912 so Maud could show here friend where she lived, looking towards Woodside. A boy stands with a two-wheeled delivery cart(?) in the distance. No parking problems then!

...and another view looking back up Duke Street. Side roads like this were not generally "made-up" and tarmacked for many years. They were dust-bowls in the summer that required damping down and quagmires of mud in the winter.

Before it was a small estate, the Mount was the name of a single house on the site. This Bathurst's card was sent by the resident (Miss Mahon, according to trade directories) to friends on Christmas Eve 1910.

AYG 42   The Mount, Aspley Guise

The 'new' Mount area also has a postcard view, from the 1960s. The original house was still there in 1954 when a grand sale was held of all the contents of owner Mrs. A. E. Winder, including a billiard table, poultry house and a 15 h.p. Daimler Shooting brake.

"Sanpine" Series.   West Hill, Aspley Guise.

Looking down West Hill. Another card with the stamp and postmark pilfered, but helpfully the writer has added the date of "Oct 24 /04" to the message. Sent by Edith to Elsie, both of whom were in Jersey.

Looking back up the hill. The Duke Street turn is in the distance. George Norman, a five-year-old, of Hazlemere, West Hill, received severe shock and abrasions when he was knocked down by a van here in 1939, but thankfully was not seriously hurt.

"Sandpine" Series. **West Street, Aspley Guise.**

Another Sandpine card, seen used as early as 1904, of Cape Cottage on the junction where Wood Lane leaves to the left, while West Hill carries on to the right. Another good indication of the state of the roadways.

West Bank Cottages are on the right as you go towards the Square. Just the kind of cottage where the ladies would sit making lace outside their front door in the bright sunshine. Picturesque, but this was long menial work for little reward.

An atmospheric view across the rooftops from behind West Bank Cottages, looking up West Hill. You can almost smell the real fires! The northern side of West Hill is still just a field here.

From an equally high vantage point on the other side of West Hill. West Bank Cottages are centre left and Cape Cottage right. West Hill runs through the middle of the picture. Card unused. Note the ivy-covered house centre...

That ivy-covered house was known as Hillside, which is written on the back of this postcard. The publisher, Lennox-Gordon, was briefly in Woburn Sands around 1909 before moving on to Chipping Norton. The house is now Giles House.

WEST STREET, ASPLEY GUISE.

An early card with a large white panel (which I have cropped) on the right for writing on, used in September 1903. The Square is just in the distance

I don't have the specific location for this house, but it is in Aspley Guise. Miss Taylor appeared at her door in an American magazine called "*The Craftsman*" in a feature on traditional British cottage lacemaking in 1912.

A rather badly-repaired advert from *"The Residential Attractions of Woburn Sands & Aspley Guise and District"* guide book of 1925. Edwin Murrer played cricket for Aspley Guise. He died in March 1951, still living at 69 West Hill.

Two more adverts from the 1903 Parish magazine. Gregory's local view postcards could be bought for just a penny each! If only…

ASPLEY GUISE
SOUVENIR PROGRAMME
OF EVENTS IN
CELEBRATION OF THE
CORONATION OF
HER MAJESTY
QUEEN ELIZABETH II

At the PARISH CHURCH of S. Botolph

Sunday, 31st May. Trinity Sunday:
6 p.m., Special Evensong (form as issued by Command of the Queen) and Sermon on the Coronation Service.

Monday, 1st June:
6 p.m. to midnight, Vigil of Thanksgiving and Prayer for our Queen and Country.

Tuesday, 2nd June:
8 a.m., The Parish Communion.
9.30 a.m., Special Service for Children.

TUESDAY, 2nd JUNE, 1953.

10 a.m. to 5 p.m.
Television of Coronation Ceremony and Procession in the Parish Hall.
5.30 p.m. Procession of Children in Fancy Dress and Decorated Vehicles form up in the Square.
5.45 p.m. Procession leaves Square for the Common.
6.30 p.m. Judging Fancy Dresses and Vehicles.
7.0 p.m. Picnics on Common.
8.0 p.m. Square Dancing on Common.
9.0 p.m. Relay of the Queen's Speech on the Common.
10.0 p.m. Processions of Torch Bearers arrive on Common and Giant Bonfire lit.

WEDNESDAY, 3rd JUNE.

2.15 p.m. onwards.—Children's Sports on the Meadows, Bedford Road, by kind permission of R. Stewart, Esq. and W. Francis, Esq.
4.0 p.m. Children's Tea.
8 p.m. to midnight. Dance in the Parish Hall for young people of the parish between 15 and 30 years of age.

FRIDAY, 5th JUNE

Afternoon.—Motor Coach Tour and Tea for Old People.

DECORATED HOUSE COMPETITION
Judging will take place on the 1st June.

The Queen Elizabeth II Coronation Programme for Aspley Guise in 1953. Another production by the local Powage Press.

THE STEAMER INN, ASPLEY GUISE.

There was another beerhouse on West Hill, the Steamer. No-one has ever explained the presence of an Anchor, a Steamer and a Swan so far from the water! The Steamer was short-lived, c.1851-1927, after which it was known as Easter Cottage for a while before the name reverted.

Lime Cottage is no.6 West Hill. Miss Ditmus is the child at the door. She used to come to Aspley Guise with her family for holidays, like here in May 1907.

Originally one house with its neighbour Ivy Cottage, they were divided in about 1817.

A sale of 1873 described it as *"Drawing and Dining Rooms, Kitchen, Scullery with hard water pump, Larder, Cellar, Four Bedrooms and two Attics, with the Yard, Stable and Loft over Coachhouse, Coal and Wood House, good Garden and appurtenances at the rear, also capital garden in front with carriage entrance, the whole being in the occupation of Captain Marriott at the yearly rental of £25".*

Miss Ditmus grew up and moved to Aspley Guise, residing here for many years. She wrote a history of St. Botolph's in 1970, which was printed by Powage Press

One of a stereo-card pair of Beal House, taken from the high bank on the opposite side of West Hill. The house itself is also one of a pair, with Cranbrook. Beal House was once known as White Cottage and had a large orchard behind it. It now has Grade II listing.

These cards present two offset images separately to the left and right eye of the viewer, giving the perception of 3D depth.

Almost back into the Square, we are looking back up West Hill at a house called Tilcocks and/or St. Andrew's Lodge. The building served as the post office until May 1916, when it moved to the three-storeyed building in Church Street. An unused Cheetham card, with a water-barrel(?) cart in the road, to help keep the dust down.

St. Andrew's Lodge Aspley Guise

With the Square immediately behind the camera, the flat-roofed addition that was the Post Office can be clearly seen. Quite a barren-looking view, in deep winter perhaps? Sent to Mr. & Mrs. Sinfield "...*and the boy*", with Christmas wishes c.1905.

Aspley Guise, West Hill

By the 1950s the old Post Office building had gone, with no evidence it was ever there. A front garden has replaced it.

ASPLEY GUISE - WOODSIDE, WOOD LANE & OTHERS

WOODSIDE, Aspley Guise.

Woodside (which fronts the Bedford Estate woodland) and Wood Lane (which connects Wood Side to West Hill), together with their sideroads, form a distinct area of Aspley Guise. Not being on a main route through the village, it is a quiet area of mainly large villa residences which have changed little in over a century. Most locals would recognise this view, even with so few distinguishing features in it. Undated but c.1920s. Certainly most of the houses here could afford a new-fangled autocar, even perhaps with a driver.

About time we saw Miss Holmes again, so here she is on Woodside, approximately between the two entrances to Mentone Avenue. Undated card.

In the other direction, at about the same spot. The writer was asking their friend if they knew where this was! Sent to Liverpool in 1913. Most of the houses cannot be seen now, as the hedges have grown too high.

Woodside, Aspley Guise   Valentines Series

We reach the junction where we will turn left into Wood Lane, but this taken from just inside the woods. Sent to Miss Tattum c/o Adnitt Bros. Drapery in Northampton. The writer lamented had waited in vain for her at the station, but she did not arrive... Sent 1911.

WOODSIDE ASPLEY GUISE

A cryptically-written card containing a series of abbreviations, in which W.W. wrote to Miss Hill that he *"did enjoy my walk through here yesterday, didn't you + hope we shall be able to explore again dear..."* in July 1911.

A Holmes card of the houses at the top of Wood Lane, looking back at the woods gate. The photographer of most of her postcards was Harold Camburn of Tunbridge Wells. He specialised in postcard views, travelling far and wide on business, but mainly on the south coast. Setting up business in 1906, he only retired in 1951.

Gregory's Sanpine Press in Woburn Sands produced a number of good views of Aspley Guise, as he had served an apprenticeship with Powage Press. Was the original name of this road changed, or did he just make a mistake? This is definitely Wood *Lane*, looking towards the woods gate. Undated card.

Further down the hill, before houses lined it both sides. Miss Holmes retired in October 1946. She died at Homeland, Wood Lane on 17th March 1970, aged 78.

This is a private drive off Wood Lane. It was once called Locarno Road, as it was laid out c.1925 when the Locarno Treaty was signed. Residents asked for it to be renamed Spinney Way in 1927, but the Council refused, as there was already a Spinney Lane. So Wayside was used until later when it became Green Lane.

Whilst we are in such wooded surrounds, there are plenty of "Aspley Guise Woods" postcards. Few places in the woods have their own specific names, but Ling Hill is one. It appears on early OS maps as a large crossroads of paths in the middle of Aspley Wood, about half-way towards the Woburn Road from the Woodside gate.

The area was once in the middle of the fuller's earth works, but has been reinstated since that closed.

An unused card c.1925, this has been in the hands of **Mr**. Yeatman's postcard shop in Hogsthorpe, Skegness in 1975, who always added a large ink-stamp of his details to the rear of his stock, irritating a lot of collectors!

"The Edge of the Wood" A Cheetham postcard sent from Aspley back home to France in 1906 by holidaymakers staying locally. Probably the reverse of the journey most postcards make now.

A portrait-orientated postcard certainly shows off the height of the local trees to maximum effect.

This was posted to Bedford in 1925 so the writer could thank their friend for suggesting a vacation in Aspley:

"I am so happy here, have never enjoyed a holiday more. It is all too beautiful to describe - thank you so much for recommending me here."

Below, the Aspley Guise Royal Antediluvian Order of Buffaloes. The RAOB started in 1822, known as "the Buffs" to members. It was set up for stage-hands at London theatres, as actors had their own social societies that such staff were not permitted to join. The only name known here is that of Percy Holmes, on the far left. This card is one of a very few with the addition of a hand-stamp to the rear of the publisher *"A. Gibbons, Aspley Guise, Beds."*

An untitled, unsent card with no publisher on, from another local collection where it was known to be the Aspley Guise Bowls Club. Their club house looks quite temporary. This was sited where the Aspley Guise Scout Hut is now, on Spinney Lane.

A SOUVENIR OF ASPLEY GUISE

Why have one view when you can have a selection? One of Blake & Edgar's Bedfordshire series of cards for economical tourists. Unsent.

I hope you have enjoyed this ramble through Woburn and Aspley Guise in vintage postcards.

This book is dedicated to the memory of Alice Holmes, seen here in 1913. Although there were plenty of other local postcard publishers, along with some national ones, who showed Aspley Guise and district, no-one else had such coverage or obvious passion for the photography.

"A presentation was made to Miss A. Holmes on Saturday… on her retirement as post mistress, a position she has held for more than thirty years in Aspley Guise and ten years in Woburn Sands. The gifts were in the form of a gold brooch set with a small diamond, and cheque for £40 10s." (Beds. Times, October 1946)

I think she would have been surprised and pleased that her images bring such fascination today, a century later.

Acknowledgements

I have drawn information from the invaluable *"Book of Woburn"*, (2nd. ed. 2000) by Kenneth Spavins and Anne Applin and *"The Story of Aspley Guise"*, (1980), by the Woburn Sands District Society. The *"Community Histories"* webpages provided by Bedfordshire Archives were extremely useful, especially during the lockdown period when archives were closed to visitors.

Some postcard images have come from the collection of the Woburn Sands & District Society archive. My grateful thanks to them.

The members of the Facebook group *"Woburn Sands and Aspley Heath History"* were always ready to identify locations and help with names and dates. Thank you all for your input.

Thanks to Bob Brown and family for providing the portrait of his aunt, Miss Alice Holmes.

I am indebted to John Clarke and Fran Fry for reading the Woburn and Aspley Guise sections respectively and providing corrections and useful additions to the text.

To the other local postcard collectors, past and present, who have generously shared what they have and know, thank you all.

Special thanks to Bryan Dunleavy at Magic Flute Publications, specialists in local history books of Milton Keynes, for the original layout and design concept.

Lastly, thank you to my understanding family who have waited patiently at endless postcard fairs while I trawl them for anything new, often finding nothing. It was all worth it!

Also by Paul Cox

Down & Needham: A Celebrated Homebrewed Success Story, 1998, Self
The Woburn Sands & Aspley Heath World War One Casualties, 2001, WSTC
The Woburn Sands Heritage Trail, 2007, WSTC
George Castleden, Bard of Woburn, 2019, Magic Flute
Milton Keynes & Area Old Flagons & Stoneware Bottles, 2020, Self
Woburn Sands, Aspley Heath & Wavendon Vintage Postcards, 2020, Magic Flute

Much of my local history research for Woburn Sands and the surrounding villages, compiled over the last 30 years, can be found online at:

www.mkheritage.org.uk/wsc

…kindly hosted by the Milton Keynes Heritage Association.